GIANT AIRLINERS

GIANT AIRLINERS

Royal Dutch Airlines

LANCE COLE

MBI Publishing Company

Dedication

For Richard and Gill Wilding, without whom I would not have flown.

Page 1: The ultimate 'Heavy' – the 747. This one is the Qantas Flight 2 arriving back at Sydney after its long haul home from London, carrying 412 passengers 12,000 miles with only one stop to refuel: a true achievement indeed.

Pages 2–3: As an Egypt Air Boeing 767 slides by, KLM's Boeing in blue rotates out of Amsterdam Schiphol. Where once, great sailing ships rode the winds, now great sky liners ruffle the airs of this reclaimed inland sea that is *Koninklijke Luchtvaart Maatschappij*'s home base.

Page 7: The elegant tail of a VASP MD-11 rests at Los Angeles during uplifts, in the background Asiana's 747-400 awaits its next task.

CONTENTS

INTRODUCTION

'Heavy' – this is the classic call out from Air Traffic Control when a big jet enters the zone and the crew call in to announce their presence. From that moment on, the big jet, its flight call sign and its ATC code, are all rounded off with the spoken word 'Heavy'. For this is the true sign that a really big airliner is on the scene; airborne small fry are suitably warned.

In past times, big jets usually had four engines, the likes of the 707, DC-8, CV-990, and VC10 were the biggest jet liners of their day and they were the true giants of the sky, the marvels of the first and second generations of the jet age. Yet the advent of the widebodied era with the arrival of the 747, DC-10 and L-1011 TriStar, saw the need for these new leviathans of the sky to be labelled and tagged for the giants that they are. Issues like wake turbulence, manoeuvring speeds and climb and descent rates all changed with the arrival of the Jumbos and the big jets – as did the logistics of handling them on the ground. Thus was born the need to identify their progress through the sky as they traversed the invisible aerial roads that are the airways that span the globe. So came into being the definition of a new type and so arrived a new call out, 'Heavy' – and a new age was born.

Since the early big jets and on through the 747-100s and -200s, on beyond the early tri-jets and now, into the age of the giant, ultra long-haul Airbus products, large airliners have held an enduring appeal for the civil aviation enthusiast. Something big on the wing always causes a stir. Aviation enthusiasts still look up to watch a 'Heavy' on finals, and then see it touch down. There is without doubt still a fascination for the very fact that these 300–400 ton monsters, manage to get airborne and climb out on another haul around the world. In *Heavies*, we follow these big jets and zoom in on the real heavy metal action that is the life and times of the biggest airliners in the world – where the acres of airframe allow livery designs to be shown to best effect.

Once, the great ocean liners were the biggest thing that could be seen; now, the big jets, the big sky liners, are the ultimate industrial leviathans. They truly are aluminium architecture – massive constructions on the move. With the advent of the 777 and Airbus A330, the 'Heavy' takes on another new form and complements what is perhaps the ultimate, quintessential 'Heavy', the grand Boeing 747 – the aircraft that changed the world. Neither must we forget that Concorde, the Ilyushin jets, and some of the bigger members of the A300 family, qualify as big jets, as true 'Heavies'.

Displayed here are some classic moments from the lives of the heavy jets as they can be seen earning their multi-million dollar keep, on the ramps, runways, and skyways of the international airline scene. In *Heavies*, the old and the new make up an essential airline album. Focus on classic 747s as they rumble in or roar off, see the flight deck action and the view from the Captain's seat; follow the new Airbus giants as they taxi up to the stand or leap off the runway. A host of airliner variants and a kaleidoscope of airline liveries are captured in *Heavies* as it stops off at major airports such as: Amsterdam, Hong Kong, Los Angeles, Heathrow, Denpasar, Sydney, Chicago, Shannon, Frankfurt, New York and others. Through the privileged, airside and flight deck access of this book you can savour the operations of big jets the world over. Ramp action and live flight deck moments are captured on line, en route, as the swept-winged giants, the new Blue Riband liners of our age, thunder onwards and upwards.

AUTHOR'S NOTE

The photographs in *Heavies* were taken by me during my work on the ramps and flight decks of the airports and airlines of the world. I hope they portray the essential essence and scale of heavy jet operations. These images would not have been captured without the kind help of many people in the airline industry. My thanks go to all of them, especially: Aer Lingus – Tom McInerney, Capt Joe Cull, Mary at Shannon, the Bryce family. The PR team at KLM. The Schiphol Airport Authority. The PR people at British Airways, Cathay Pacific, Qantas, Garuda Indonesia, Shannon Airport, Sydney Airport, and to all who helped along the airways. The photographs were taken on Canon EOS cameras and lenses, using Fuji and Kodak professional films. Thanks are due to the people at Airlife Publishing for making books.

Lance Cole

Cockwood Harbour, Devon England

Opposite: 'Heavy' hauler, a Thai Airbus A300 curves round the bend at Kai Tak as the sun sets. Note the long span slats and flaps.

Above: A Garuda DC-10 about to launch from the beachside runway at Bali's Denpasar airport.

747 – QUEEN OF THE SKIES

This is the big one, the aeroplane that really began the 'Heavy' label. See a 747 emerge from the clouds, turn, select gear down and sink in on final approach with its massive flaps dangling, and its sheer 'Heavy' appeal is obvious. Watch one gracefully climb away and pack its eighteen wheels up into their holds, and you will be in no doubt that you are in the presence of something special – a double-decked airframe of massive proportions that has never been copied nor eclipsed.

The 747, through its initial -100 model, then the -200 (Super B) variant, and on into the extended upper deck -300 version, truly captures the spirit of the massive airliner. Add in winglets, uprated engines, revised structures and a CRT flight deck and the -400 version of the 747 becomes the true ruler of the airways in terms of size and sheer visual presence.

Originally conceived in the mid-1960s under a $2 billion risk venture by Boeing, with design input from Pan Am, the 20 ft wide cabin and double-decked seating configuration created the first true widebody airliner – an aircraft twice as large as its 707 ancestor. The early variants had a max take-off weight of 710,000 lb/310,000 kg, with the latest -400 hurtling into the air at 870,000 lb/395,000 kg – well over 300 tons, and, fully fuelled, nearer 400 tons – still a staggering figure. The shorter-bodied SP had an extended range but higher operating costs. The 747 Combi offers real adaptability for airlines with its mix of cargo and passengers – especially in -300 EUD variant – which KLM has used so effectively. KLM has also created the rare 'one off', add-on extended upper deck of the -300 model to some of its early short topped -200 fleet.

With a typical cabin layout of 412 seats, yet over 500 being fitted into the Japanese market 747SR series, the 747 can back up its heavy metal claims. Indeed, the 747 holds the world record for passenger uplift when 630 passengers (and no luggage!) were crammed into a Qantas 747-200 during the emergency evacuation of Darwin during a natural cyclone disaster in the 1970s.

The globe-trotting 747-400 carries nearly 60,000 gallons of fuel and can fly from London to Sydney with only one stop en route. (A Qantas 747-400 flew London–Sydney non-stop on its non revenue delivery flight, a world record that stood until a globe-circling A340 took the crown several years later.) Equipped with crew rest bunks and a roof-mounted crew rest compartment, the two pilot equipped -400, with onboard self-navigation equipment (FANS), can carry itself and its tail-plane mounted extra fuel capacity for 7,500 miles.

Naturally, the American operators made the 747 their own, with Pan Am, TWA, United, Northwest, and a host of famous names heading the 747 roll call, yet such was the impact of the 747, that everyone had to have one. Of course, the likes of BOAC/BA, KLM Lufthansa, Alitalia, SAS, Sabena, Qantas, JAL, Air France, et al, all bought the 747, but so too did less well known carriers like Nigeria Airways, Air Maroc and Cameroon Airlines. Second-hand 747s filtered down to the charter market and into the hands of smaller airlines. The simple fact was that the 747 as the true widebodied giant, could not be beaten for years.

To the pilot, 747s handle like a dream, well balanced and with smooth action, they can be made to glide serenely along or turn and climb away with real pace. On the approach, much stability is on offer allowing vital decision-making time in the landing profile. The early Pratt & Whitney power-plants have been uprated and the General Electric and Rolls-Royce engine options have opened up a new chapter for the 747.

Rumbling through the sky like giant paddle steamers, with the engines churning and the air billowing over their vast bodies, the 747s really do make a majestic progress. The Cathedral-like feel of a 747's vast wings, fin and fuselage as one walks under it, are fitting tribute to the reverence this design achievement deserves. Regal and yet a plane of the people – for whom the 747 offered cheap travel – the juggernaut 747 changed history.

The sheer size of the 747 is rarely appreciated by passengers as they board or de-plane via sealed jetways that hide the 747 from them. Yet seen from the ramp, or even better from the air, the 747 really makes its leviathan mark on the senses. The sheer acreage of panels, the extent of the plating and structure, the towering fin, all of this really does remind one of a giant ship, a great liner – which is of course, just what the mighty 747 is.

Tokyo by night. Classic 747s at JAL's home airport await their next long haul. In the foreground a 747-300, behind, the classic 747-200 model.

Above: ANZ One. Arriving at Heathrow after ranging up from New Zealand via Los Angeles, this 747-400 makes a spectacular sight in the early morning light.

Opposite above: 'Heavy' Captain. After years of toil pilots get the four gold stripes and the wisdom to go with them. Here, a senior Qantas Captain – Captain Hughes, finishes his pre-flight walk-around his sky liner and makes ready to pilot her to Australia from London Heathrow.

Opposite below: The long way back; Qantas QF002 rumbles in after twenty-one hours on the wing from London to Sydney, whilst another example of the 'Longreach' class rests up. Longreach is the name of the founding home town of Qantas – in Australia's farming heartland where the airline had its beginnings in the 1920s.

Heading home, SAA's multi-hued 747-300 leaps out of London. The
Pratt & Whitneys are pumping at full power as close to 400 tonnes
heads on out. In ten hours time it will ease itself down through an
African dawn and arrive in Johannesburg.

Clean-lined climb-out. Virgin's 747-400 G-VTOP gets the gear packed away and the climb angle correct as LAX slips away beneath. Virgin has a mixed fleet of 747-400s, -200s and Airbus A340s.

Opposite above: Air-India 747 on finals. Inbound 747-400 action as a cross-wind slaps at the fin and tries to weathercock the big Boeing around.

Opposite below: Winglets at dawn. Cathay Pacific's 747-400s vie for space at the old Hong Kong Kai Tak. To the rear a venerable 747-200F cargo craft looks majestically on whilst the composite fibre winglets mirror each other's range-enhancing design.

Above: Old 747s go on for ever. This ex-Pan Am machine was being fettled by Qantas at Sydney prior to sale by its owner to another carrier. With the aft cowling removed, the inner workings of the mid and end core stages of the classic Pratt & Whitney JT9 are revealed.

A British Airways 747-400 scythes around the bend into Kai Tak during the last days of the airport. A sudden downdraft and cross-wind gust hit this aircraft just after she had made the 47-degree turn. The pilot is in the process of correcting the skid and drift and watching the sink rate – all at once – really earning his money.

Classic arrival as a Rolls-Royce RB211 D4-equipped 747-200 curves
into Kai Tak – 'Heavy' perfection?

Los Angeles ramp scene – SIA's Megatop 747-400 9V-SPC takes on fuel, food and folks prior to start-up and another Pacific crossing.

Opposite above: Air Namibia's 747 SP hurries out of Frankfurt. Note the simplified wing flaps and shorter fuselage of this, the higher flying, longer-ranged early model of the 747 family.

Opposite below: Pacific dawn. On board Cathay Pacific as the ultra long-haul flight number CX800 great circles its way from Hong Kong to San Francisco, whilst the analogue dials glow and the Captain sits on guard as the blue skyscape blazes.

An All Nippon Airways 747-400 gets into the groove. Note the wing flex under take-off load.

Asiana's 747-400 at LAX. This young airline now spreads far and wide – having truly earned its stripes – as seen in the unusual colour scheme.

Climb-out – 12 degrees on the attitude indicator, gear just yanked up
and the fuel flow racing as Japan Airlines displays pure 747 power.

Coming into Hong Kong during Kai Tak days, this JAL 747-200 oozes with intent. The massive flaps and multi-axle gear are well displayed.

A Flying Tigers 747 freighter sinks into London Heathrow with plenty of power to prevent the higher landing weight from developing a high sink rate. With her Pratts screaming and the vast unpainted acres of plating straining, this grand old lady of a freighter has seen it all.

In-flight delight; the view most passengers get through the windows of a 'Heavy'.

Opposite: The distinctive face of the 747 (KLM style) on the ramp at Schiphol where the blue birds nest between flights. Note the windscreen wipers and the peaked upper deck shape – slightly different from the shorter-topped, non-extended upper-deck design of the earlier models. The EUD design confers a small aerodynamically tuned advantage.

Right: The sheer scale of things captured as the ground crew chief unplugs his radio link to the flight deck and the KLM 747-400 makes ready with her General Electric powerplants throbbing away.

Below: Full flap, 150 knots, ease the nose up a touch and this KLM 747-400 will cream onto the runway at Bali airport. Note the triple slotted flap design at full extension.

Above: One of the China Airlines fleet screams into Kai Tak in some near marginal visual conditions. Note the vortices streaming off the wings.

Opposite: Cathay Pacific's Rolls-Royce RB211 524s sit and brood under a sullen Hong Kong sky as the wing tanks are topped up with fuel and an engineer inspects a jet pipe.

Below: One of the original British Airways 747-100s in classic repose as she creeps up to the take-off hold point on LHR's 27R on a wet and windy day. The BA livery lends an elegant air to the proceedings. These early machines, which once wore the elegant BOAC blue and gold paint scheme, have now been pensioned off and turned into scrap.

Opposite above: Garuda Indonesia's venerable old workhorse 747-200 PK-GSE waddles out to the runway in the heat of an Indonesian afternoon.

Opposite below: The 747-400 brought the 'glass' cockpit to the 747 and here we see some actual in-flight action on-board the QF001 en route from London to Sydney. Note the waypoints and track on the navigation screen, and engine EPR and fuel flow details on the centre screen.

Above: Middle East Airlines – but the famous Cedar Tree is adorning an American-registered craft as this 747 punts along very nicely thank you.

Above: Despite an attempt at a more modern livery, Air-India reverted to its traditional scheme – even on its latest 747-400s – this one is rumbling out of Heathrow on its way to warmer climes.

Opposite above: Touchdown! Air-India arrives at Frankfurt on a summer's evening in the form of this 747-200 which was fairly racing along as it caught the setting sun.

Opposite below: Classic stuff: one of the earlier, second batch of Lufthansa 747-200s – which replaced the airline's original 747-100 models – makes ready to depart Frankfurt in the 1980s heyday of Lufthansa's classic old colour scheme. All polished metal and fresh paint, she epitomises the high standards of the airline.

747 sunset – the unmistakable silhouette of the 747's fin captured on
a sweaty summer's evening at Chicago.

AIRBUS A330/340 – THE NEW CLASSICS

With the A330 and A340 airframes, Airbus Industrie expanded their themes and conquered even more sky space. The four-engined A340, with its high aspect ratio design, winglets and long body, hints at past shapes from the DC-8-60 series and the 707, yet at the same time advances the art of the airliner. With ultra-efficient aerofoil section wings, framed by elegant winglets equipped with computerised, side-stick controls, the A340 is a fuel miser and long-range luxury liner all rolled into one. First premiered by Lufthansa back in 1993, the A340 still looks fresh and in the -200 variant can fly over 7,000 nautical miles. The rare, one-off VIP A340-800 added a thousand miles to that range. The -200 model can be spotted by its slightly nose-down stance. The extended-body -300 model sacrifices little for its extra carrying capacity, with up to 300 souls being accommodated (50 or so more than the -200). With over 50,000 lb of cargo load and a 588,800 lb/253,500 kg max take-off weight, the A340-300 represents an awesome sight in the sky.

Today, the A340/330 family has sold so well that, along with other airbus types, the firm has overtaken Boeing as the leading supplier to the world's airlines. From Virgin to Kuwait Airways, from Thai to Austrian, from airlines on every continent, long-range A340/330s wing in every morning to the world's leading airports.

The A330 is closely modelled upon the A340 airframe but sees a revised wing with the two outboard engines deleted – thus creating the elegant lines of arguably the best-looking of the big twin jets. Powered by two CFM turbofans, the A330 in -200 and -300 versions can be used on transoceanic long hauls and on medium and long-range inter-city services carrying up to 335 passengers at Mach 0.86. Airlines like Aer Lingus and Cathay Pacific are at the forefront of building up A330 over-ocean flying hours.

The uninterrupted mid to outboard slats, efficient flaps and tuned wings convey excellent hot and high characteristics and the aircraft is consequently very popular with tropical zone operators. The close commonality between the A330 and A340 means that pilots can train to fly both with minimal revisions and with near identical dimensions, the aircraft handle remarkably similarly. The A330 however, weighs in with a max take-off weight of 467,379 lb/ 212,000 kg. Both share a span of 197.83 ft/ 60.30 m. With advanced composite fibre construction, fly-by-wire systems and advanced flight management equipment, the A340 and A330 really do fly at the leading edge of efficiency.

Elegance exemplified as an Aer Lingus A330 pushes back in big twin style.

Opposite: A330 *St Brigid* awaits start-up clearance at Shannon. Note the clean lines, wing box design and flush-finished fuselage – all essential drag-reducing ingredients. The Irish airline operates five A330-300s and two A330-200s.

Above and below: With the winglet angle well shown, this A330 poses for the camera in these two views of ramp action. Observe the long span slats and heavy-duty gear.

Opposite: A330 EI-DUB awaits uplift in this winglet portrait. The aerodynamic fine tuning – reducing drag and tailoring wing vortices – of these composite construction devices adds notable lift and range components to the overall wing aerofoil performance. The 'canoe' fairings of the flap tracks are also visible.

Above: Airbus atmosphere as the A330 trundles off the ramp while behind some old 707s sit and watch the world go by from their retirement park at Shannon airport!

Below: Lift-off. As the A330 howls down the runway under computer controlled, side-sticked command, the wings grab the air at rotate speed and she's off across the Atlantic to JFK. Aer Lingus pioneered over-ocean ETOPS hour building with its A330s from 1995 onwards.

Here we see the stand-by analogue dial instruments as well as the CRT-displayed status of EI-CRK as she rests.

Opposite above: Steady as she goes on the climb out.

Opposite below: The six CRT screens and FMS console of the A330 flight deck – similar to the A340 to allow dual crewing.

Opposite: The flight management system, ECAM controls and mode select, plus throttles and inertial navigation system are simplified and easy to assimilate. The lower screen is showing the fuel status.

Left: From the Captain's seat – a simple and clear view.

Below: The front cabin of an Aer Lingus A330 as the crew take a short break between flights.

Main cabin on the Aer Lingus A330 – eight seats across, with plenty of room.

Aer Lingus, like KLM, has stuck to its distinctive and established livery. Here the shamrock and green are colourfully captured.

Opposite above: Kuwait Airways was an early A340 customer, here one of its 340s roars off into a hot and smoggy sky. Note the elevator angle – holding the aircraft in perfect pitch whilst the wings flex under load and the engines paddle away.

Opposite below: Air Canada's Airbus A340 cruises out to the launch point on Heathrow's northerly runway on a gloomy winter's day. The airline operates a mixed fleet of 767s and A340s across the Atlantic.

Baby 'Heavy' – Royal Jordanian's exquisitely-liveried A310 makes a refuelling stop at Shannon en route from Amman to New York. By stopping off at Shannon, the airline avoids the congestion of major European airports. Note the wingtip fence – a 'mini' winglet that tunes tip vortexes but does not have a lift component.

Above: Another baby 'Heavy'. Packed with German tourists, this Hapag-Lloyd Airbus A310 is heading out from Ireland en route to the Caribbean over the Atlantic wastes under big twin ETOPS rules.

Opposite above: Airbus art as an A310 takes off.

Opposite below: A rainy day in London for this Virgin Atlantic A340 as it taxies out to its launch point. You can see the wings taking the heavy fuel load and the centre body-gear doing likewise. The logo on the rear of the fuselage refers to Mr Branson's battle with a certain airline.

Above: Air Lanka's A340 leaps away as the thrust gets into the groove for this Columbo-bound beauty.

Opposite above: Wearing the earlier Egypt Air colours, another A340 hauls out in classic 'Heavy' repose and displays the A340's amazing degree of wing flex.

Opposite below: Homecoming. After fourteen hours on the wing with only one stop, Lufthansa's A340 nudges up to the gate at Frankfurt after arriving from Santiago de Chile and Argentina on the airline's longest haul. Note the large spacing between inboard and outboard engines.

An A340 composite tail frames the Lufthansa home base legend. Note the fin support structure and moulded fairing at the fin-to-fuselage join.

Above: American Airlines uses A300s all over its route network.
Heathrow normally sees 767s from AA; on this occasion the airline
used an A300 to cross the pond.

Below: Air-India uses A310s on intra-Asian routes. This sprightly
A310 is wheeling around the Hong Kong bend as it straightens up to
sink into Kai Tak.

Opposite above: The Virgin Airbus parking lot at LHR – seen from the flight deck of another Airbus as it exits runway 27L.

Opposite below: Stunning silhouette – An A340 throttled back under an early morning sky as she wafts in on finals.

Above: Garuda Indonesia used early model A300s. Here a GE-powered B4 model in the revised colours sits and sweats at Kai Tak prior to heading off back down the map to Jakarta.

Opposite: With Pan Am's classic 'Heavies' behind it, this Pan Am A310 is getting ready to load up and haul out in the carrier's last, great days.

Below: Nose art in the form of the A330's contours.

BOEING BIG TWINS – TRIPLE SEVENS AND SEVEN SIXES

It took a very long time for the airlines to accept that you could fly the Atlantic on just two engines. As long ago as 1956, the British Vickers company drew up plans for a transatlantic-ranged airliner with three engines, yet the airlines still insisted on having four engines for decades afterwards. Indeed, in some contexts, the so-called 'big twin' debate still rumbles on. Meanwhile, after a change in attitude and after grasping the improved economics of such a twin-jet powered concept, the 'big twin' idea is now accepted. Certainly the fuel crisis era and the advent of really big turbo fans that could operate reliably with very low shutdown rates, combined with advanced electronic flight management systems, ushered in a new age. Now, many airlines are racking up extended-range operations with large, twin-engined airliners. The height of Boeing's big twin concept is the 777 or 'triple seven' as the aircraft seems to often be called. Yet the groundwork for such operations was laid in the late 1980s and early 1990s by the 767 family.

In 767-200 form, the first Boeing big twin weighs in at 300,000 lb/136,078 kg max take-off weight with a 3,670 nm/ 5,905 km range; the longer-bodied -300ER model achieves a 345,000 lb/156,500 kg max take-off weight with near 6,000 mile range.

With the ability to carry 250 passengers in -300 form and 210 in the -200 version, the 767s offer impressive seat/mile costs. Airlines like Trans World, Air Canada and EL AL did much of the early EROPS/ETOPS over-water twin-powered groundwork. As late as 1999, airlines were selling off other types and switching to 767s – indeed, 767 operator American Airlines decided to phase out MD-11 tri-jets on its European services and replace them with 767s.

Gradually with special systems enhancements and a growing record for safe running, the big fan-engined, big twin 767s made aviation authorities extend the allowed range from diversion or alternate airfields. From a 90-minute alternate starting point, to today's 180-minute diversion range (with 210 minutes proposed), the big twin concept seems to have won the argument.

To prove the point, Boeing launched its 777. As long as a 747, and powered by two giant turbo fans of General Electric or Rolls-Royce design, the massive 777 was the first fly-by-wire Boeing. With a massive 6,000-mile plus range, huge 350 plus seating capacity and advanced construction allied to a super efficient aerofoil section, the 777 is the biggest and boldest example yet of the big twins. With its globe-circling range, wide cabin and enormous engines, all supported by a multi-axle main gear, the 777 simply shouts 'Heavy' and is perhaps the ultimate twin-powered big jet.

An Emirates 777 thunders away. Observe the multi-axle main gear and high aspect ratio wing that can be seen flexing under load; this is the biggest 'big twin' – especially in the -300 IGW increased weight variant.

Opposite: The 777 was Boeing's first fly-by-wire airframe. The aerodynamics were also advanced – note the end-plate type tail cone and thin fin design. This 777 depicts one of the British Airways multi-ethnic fin liveries.

Opposite above: United's mega twin 777 taxies in as the huge engine cowlings and sharp fin shape mark out the 777 design motifs. The fuel miser 777 is ideal for United's flights from the west and east coast of America across the Atlantic to Europe.

Opposite below: Royal Brunei uses its attractively-painted 767-300s between Brunei and Europe. Note the broader tail fin in comparison with the 777 profile – making it easy to tell the two types apart at a distance.

Above: Heavy arrival – 777 silhouette as the big jet steadies on finals. Note the triple-axle gear design.

Above: The Star Alliance Group of airlines are displayed on this SAS-operated 767 in its unusual livery. To the rear is a 'Heavy' parking lot.

Opposite: Avianca *(above)* ranges far and wide with its 767s. The livery strikes a classic if dated look, whilst *(below)*, Uzbekistan Airlines' more modern hues adorn its 767. Both give the spotters something to think about at Heathrow.

KLM Royal Dutch Airlines replaced its A310s with 767s and uses the big Boeing on intra-European and Middle-Eastern routes. Captured during a fly-by, this one displays the stunning KLM blue that is perhaps the best and most timeless livery design of all.

Seen in the carrier's older livery, this is VARIG's short-bodied 767 about to leave London for Rio de Janeiro in a blur of blue and white.

Above: Boeing 767 tails glint as a 777 climbs out in the background. To the fore, the sharp fin of a Kuwait Airways 777 adds to the moment.

Opposite above: Gulf Air built up its international routes with the VC10, consolidated them with the TriStar, and then made them even more efficient by using the 767. This one is cantering into Kai Tak on a sticky afternoon – a real 767-300ER moment.

Opposite below: Airframe detail – Air New Zealand's 767 shows off its big slat angle and traditional Boeing nose as it taxies at Denpasar, Bali.

Opposite above: Qantas uses a fleet of 767s on Australian and Asian services. One of them holds the world record for the shortest jet airline flight when it suffered a bird strike on take off and with one engine out and the other damaged, it made an emergency landing a few short minutes later – back where it started! This 767 is seen at rest behind the Rolls-Royce RB211 524 engine of a Qantas 747-400 at Sydney.

Opposite below: Air Canada was a 767 pioneer. Here a -200 model cleaves out of Toronto's Lester D Pearson airport. The 'seven six' is rock steady on the climb-out and the gear is just coming up.

Above: Alitalia was a later customer of the 767 – putting it to good use on a diverse set of routes. This one is visiting Amsterdam with a heavy load of travellers.

American Airlines detail. A huge fleet of 767s in -200 and -300 guise range far and wide for AA. Some head off to Latin America, others cross the Atlantic many times a day and make ETOPS what it is.

Leaving Frankfurt, this 767-300ER is heading off for another Mach 0.85 cruise across the pond under twin-engined rules as its 345,000 lb/156,000 kg lumbers up into the sky.

Glinting in the heat, this view of the all-metal finish that American Airlines uses, seems to lengthen the aircraft's lines. With the advent of the further stretched 767-400, such a stretched look to the 767 is not as odd as it might appear.

Opposite: The 757 used the 767-style windscreen frame – albeit faired into a narrower fuselage crown and married to a very untraditional-shaped nose for a Boeing. Seen here is the fatter profile of the 767 in head-on view as this United 767 glistens on the ramp.

THE TRI-JET HEAVIES

Alongside the 747, it is surely correct to say that the DC-10 and L-1011 are true classics, and also true 'Heavies'. They are the quintessential classic widebodies.

The DC-10 and the L-1011 have been around for a very long time. Notably, one airline was behind the specification for the DC-10, for it was American Airlines and its own engineers who set the scene for the DC-10 and who worked with Douglas to create the first widebodied tri-jet.

Inherent in the concept was the additional safety factor of a third engine, and the spare potential its inclusion in the design created for increasing weights and range above the basic airframe design outline. The fact that the domestic/transcontinental model DC-10-10 was developed into the long-range intercontinental DC-10-30/40 models underlines the success of the design. With a 550,000 lb/251,740 kg max take-off weight and a 6,160 nm/9,910 km range, and 250-seat cabin, the ultimate DC-10 was a very useful tool indeed. It remained so, and was in service for over twenty years, and despite a bad patch when it suffered a series of hull losses, was a favoured tool by many airlines. In the 1980s, the DC-10 was modernised and turned into the revised MD-11 aircraft. Strangely, despite a fuselage stretch, the tail plane was scaled down – thus affecting control authority, but much reducing drag and weight – the previous DC-10 tailplane being a large, area-ruled structure. With a 300+ seat cabin, and 5,000 nm/8,700 km range, allied to a winglet-equipped wing, the MD-11 was a useful machine, yet was soon eclipsed by the 777. The MD-11 lives on as a freighter and will also remain in passenger service with those airlines with whom it

Classic memories: CP Air's *Empress of Amsterdam* – seen appropriately at Amsterdam Schiphol. All CP Air's DC-10s followed their DC-8 forefathers in being named in the 'Empress' series. The famous orange livery has now gone.

This CP Air DC-10-30 is seen in the change-over style of livery – still painted orange but with Canadian Pacific titles and a revised livery nose-cone tacked on for effect. This one was howling into Toronto on a cold Canadian evening.

remains popular. The likes of KLM, Swissair, Thai, Iberia, Pakistan International, Lufthansa, and British Airways (which inherited its DC-10s on buying British Caledonian), were all typical foreign users of this all-American tri-jet.

Entering service way back in 1972, the DC-10 was not just a heavy tri-jet, but also the forefather of an inter-city, widebodied airbus-type concept. With its angular lines and high mounted tail engine, it became a symbol of the big tri-jet age.

Lockheed's L-1011 or TriStar, was an aircraft that came from a different concept, yet which came to serve various needs after Lockheed lost the race to prove a 747-type 'jumbo' airliner. Proficient in large structures via its C-5A Galaxy aircraft experience, the firm came up with an elegant tri-jet of its own. The L-1011, or TriStar as it became known, was less of a bullish beast than the DC-10 and more of a sleek dolphin – in looks at least. Unlike the bluff and angular DC-10, the L-1011 featured a tail-mounted engine that was buried in the rear fuselage and which was fed by an 'S' duct. With a large, curved cockpit area and engines spaced further out on the wings, the L-1011 was more graceful to look at and with its sole option engine choice of Rolls-Royce RB211 engines, handled like a dream. The L-1011 pioneered early fly-by-wire electronic type control actuation and also had a

better, hot and high airfield performance than its rivals – due to a more efficient slat and those Rolls-Royce engines. The early versions carried 250 passengers and crew over a 4,640 nm/7,470 km range. The aerodynamically-tweaked, shorter-bodied -500 ranged over 5,000 miles and still carried 230 passengers.

Modified into various versions, notably the -500 series, the L-1011, served in various US and international roles. On one hand it was a transcontinental airbus type, on another an inter-city 'whisper jet'; in other arenas the L-1011 was a true long-haul 'Heavy' that served with distinction and became popular with pilots. British pilots thought that the L-1011 almost rivalled the affection they had had for the old VC10. At Cathay Pacific the L-1011 also found a favoured home, with the airline making the most of the type and going on to buy up the Eastern Airlines L-1011 fleet. Early in its career, the L-1011 was also operated by Pan Am – alongside a fleet of DC-10s – a rare and curious tri-jet blend for one airline.

Unlike the DC-10, the L-1011 has not found favour as a freighter and it ceased production. Many elegant examples remain in service today.

Opposite: Hong Kong 'Heavies'. JAL called this a DC-10-40LR – perhaps going over the top a little to mark the differing engine option, revised fin intake shape and extra tankage. As you can see from her stance, this 'Big Ten' is loaded with fuel and passengers and is about to blast off back to Narita.

Above: Finnair used the long-range DC-10 to great effect – flying the Siberian short-cut route long before most airlines. This blue and white liveried DC-10 is trotting across the rain-soaked ramp at Singapore Changi.

Opposite above: VARIG's stunning new colour scheme and tail logo seen on one of the airline's DC-10s as it frames the ramp action at a busy Heathrow.

Opposite below: Continental operated the DC-10 from Tokyo to Guam on its Micronesian services. This is Tokyo by night as the big tri-jet awaited its task at 2300hrs.

Above: Swerving around the turn over Hong Kong, a Malaysian Airlines DC-10-30 arrives at Kai Tak. The large flaps, long span tailplane and consequent superb handling of the DC-10 are captured.

The same aircraft taxies in with the runway approach lights in the foreground.

Continental ranged far afield and here one of the airline's DC-10s
hacks into a rainy Sydney – with the city skyline as a backdrop to
arrival from across the Pacific.

Opposite above: The bright hues of the Ghana DC-10 as she steps up the climb angle and powers away en route to Accra, a stylish 'Heavy Ten' memory.

Opposite below: Now pensioned off, one of KLM's DC-10-30s creeps up to the gate at Toronto and displays its pure Douglas lineage. This view shows off the steeply raked centre windscreen and carved nose contours, under which lurks a titanium tub.

Above: VARIG's new colours adorn the airline's venerable DC-10 at LHR. MD-11s have now taken over.

Above: Viasa's DC-10 thunders through a murky sky.

Opposite above: Bangladesh Airlines turns into the sunset on Heathrow's 27L. The huge area of the tailplane on the DC-10 – reduced on the MD-11 – is clearly seen.

Opposite below: CP Air is now known as Canadian, but at least a vestige of the old orange colours was kept. This is a true 'Heavy' at rest on the ramp at Amsterdam.

An Alitalia MD-11 caught as she climbs out. Note the winglets and reduced-area tailplane – which offers less elevator authority than that of its forebear the DC-10.

An American Airlines MD-11 poses its silvered body for the camera.
Note the sheer presence of the beast.

Above: Thai's MD-11 slams down and thrust reverses at Bali whilst a Merpati F27 watches.

Below: Garuda Indonesia leased three MD-11s. This one is skimming into Bali Denpasar – hot and heavy.

Opposite: The drag-reducing winglets first seen on the 747-400 also appear on the MD-11 – although in a different design. This is the in-flight view – it is as if the winglets are sailing along beside the aircraft for the ride. Several have been ground off in wingtip strikes upon landing.

One of the Air Canada TriStar fleet caught with the long body of a DC-8F running behind it. In the background, another TriStar basks in this 1980s time warp.

A BA TriStar makes ready to roll. Note the revised intake fairing – as seen on the -500 model. A classic L-1011 'Heavy' memory.

Above: TriStar magic. Caught as she slips serenely into Kai Tak, this Cathay Pacific Super TriStar captures the type's elegance compared with the more brutal lines of its Douglas rival.

Opposite above: Air Lanka and All Nippon Airways TriStars at rest at Tokyo Narita – two diverse TriStar operators.

Opposite below: The late King Hussein's specially modified -500 TriStar. Note the anti-missile chaff tubes and ECM pods and communications addenda.

Forgotten themes, one of the All Nippon fleet of TriStars gets ready to roll at a murky Kai Tak.

Some of the British Airways TriStar fleet were originally ordered to a BEA specification, hence G-BEAK, whilst others came under the BA aegis. British Airways and its pilots loved the TriStar – building up a team spirit that aped the old days of the BOAC/BA VC10 fleet. Here the dolphin-like nose of the TriStar is profiled, whilst (*opposite*) the smoothly faired-in, S-ducted tail, marks out the main difference in engine installation compared with the DC-10. Care had to be taken with high power take-off settings not to blanket the centre intake and cause engine airflow problems. The sight of a pile of fan blades sticking out of a TriStar's tail pipe usually gave the game away!

One of Cathay Pacific's Super TriStar fleet starts its take-off roll from Kai Tak. Often heavily laden, these aircraft formed the core of Cathay Pacific's Far East growth in passenger numbers. The airline also bought up the ex-Eastern Airlines TriStar fleet and re-built the aircraft for Asian use.

CLASSIC HEAVIES

Beyond the confines of the established types seen and accepted as 'Heavy' jets, there is a host of airframe types that qualifies for the name. Even Concorde, that delicately styled, yet immensely powerful aircraft, qualifies as a 'Heavy'– its shape perhaps defying its 408,000 lb/185,060 kg max take-off weight and 100-seat range over 3,800 nm/6,223 km with supersonic speeds.

The Ilyushin -86 and -96 four-engined widebodies from the Russian design bureau also qualify as true 'Heavies' and can be seen at many international destinations. Indeed, the Il-96 with a 480,000 lb/219,000 kg max take-off weight and 6,000 nm/9,000 km range, is a 'Heavy' jet in every way – with its revised engines, winglets and large lower deck passenger loading door, it is an impressive airliner.

Throw in Antonovs and 747 freighters and the world of 'Heavies' is a colourful and huge album of great airline transport moments. Amid all these aircraft, from 747 to Il-96, we see the true achievement of our love affair with big transport aircraft and the culmination of the efforts of designers, engineers, airlines and crews, in the operation of the world's big jets – the HEAVIES.

Concorde's slim elegance shines through, even on the ground. Somehow she does not seem to look like a 'Heavy', but she is. This

Concorde is seen in the newer BA colours whilst visiting the RIAT air show.

Opposite: Wearing the old and the new BA colours, these two views show Concorde with nose at take-off setting, thrusting along with her Olympus jets at full pelt. Four engines, 100 passengers, unique climb and descent rates, a supersonic 55,000 ft cruise; of course it's a 'Heavy' jet.

Above: Russian 'Heavy' – Ilyushin 96 on finals. Note the closely coupled engines – very different from the A340's layout. Note the winglets and centre body gear – all clues to a 'Heavy' design.

A Swissair 747-300 hauls out of Geneva into the setting sun.

Air-India's briefly tried replacement livery.

Old 'Heavy' – a Saudia 707F staggers up from LHR's runway 9R.

An even older 'Heavy' – Rich International short-body DC-8 at Toronto.

Opposite above: Pan Am memories. With a fleet of over thirty 747s, Pan Am was a haven for 'Heavies' – especially the early 747-100. This one is at Paris CDG and had the air of a venerable old tramp steamer.

Above: This Middle-Eastern VIP flight 747SP model has real presence on the ramp, displaying the classic 747 nose shape and pylon-equipped wings.

Opposite below: Air-India sinks into Singapore with Pratts throttled back, flaps at 25 degrees and 160 knots on the clock.

Aerolineas Argentinas 747-200 Super B model in the airline's attractive livery as it negotiates the taxiways at Amsterdam Schiphol.

Above: Pakistan Airways is replacing its fleet of two-decade-old 747-200s. Until the new aircraft arrive, three old stagers are still hard at work. This one, Toronto-bound from Shannon, is rotating in fine style.

Below: 'Heavy' family album. Boeing 707, 767 and 747s seen at work. The airport is Tokyo Narita, the image a classic 'Heavy' memory.

Magic moments. Sunset on the QF2 – as Qantas heads home from London for an evening arrival in Sydney twenty-one hours, but two time-zoned days later. Captain Howells is in command as the skyscape blazes away in front of the 747-400.

Above: Antonov 124 – a real 'Heavy' cargo lifter basks its giant weight and wheels on Irish soil. Note the anhedral wing and conventional tailplane design. This one, operated in a joint deal with Air Foyle, is based at Shannon.

Above and left: The -200 model Antonov 124 is to be equipped with Rolls-Royce engines and a 'glass' cockpit. This 124-100 model was on a sales tour in 1999 – at the RIAT air show.

Heavy landing – a British Airways 747-400 skims in over Heathrow's approach lighting at the end of another day's heavy hauling.

SPs at sunset. Two United 747SPs meet and greet each other at Narita – both having crossed the vast Pacific.